PERSPECTIVE

How to Develop the Mindset to Start and Build Your Business

Kwabena Obeng Darko

Published by

ODTR✸H

Odtrah Publications
P. O. Box KN 5668
Kaneshie-Accra.

Email: odtrah@outlook.com
Mobile: 026 8109787 /024 6631874

Printed in Ghana By ODTRAH

For your personal copy of this book, information about other books by the author or bulk purchase please contact:

Mobile: 026 8109787 /024 6631874
Email: odtrah@outlook.com

DEDICATION

I dedicate this book to all innovators and entrepreneurs who believe in the prosperity of Africa and are committed to work it.

AUTHOR'S NOTES AND ACKNOWLEDGMENTS

It has been a lifelong journey of learning. I have made many mistakes and have had some wins as well. To all the people who have contributed to my being here, I say thank you very much. I say a big thank you to my family and friends.

A special thank you to my wife, the entrepreneur, my business partner, my greatest support, I say thank you, Marie. Lastly, to my children, Yaa, Awura and Kwabena, you are all special.

PERSPECTIVE

How to Develop the Mindset to Start
and Build Your Business

Kwabena Obeng Darko

CONTENTS

Dedication
Acknowledgement
Introduction

Chapter One:
Perspective 1

Chapter Two:
Mindset 9

Chapter Three:
Educational Foundation 13

Chapter Four:
The Relevance of History 21

Chapter Five:
Vision and Team 29

Chapter Six:
Leadership and Character 37

Chapter Seven:
Believe It 45

Chapter Eight:
Start 51

Chapter Nine:
Different Time 55

Chapter Ten:
Essential 59

After word 65

INTRODUCTION

Starting a business demands so much time and energy. It will take you years to develop the business and the leadership skills required to scale it, especially when you start with little business experience and connections. We go through this process to develop the right skills and the network needed for growth. School does not train people to start businesses. The best school can do is to prepare you for a job. At the moment, the structure of our education does not prepare students to be independent in thinking. Entrepreneurship is a school on its own, which largely is at variance with traditional school.

We are at the precipice of an increasing rate of unemployment among the people that are coming out of our universities, which is indicative of the kind of education that is being offered.

You will have to be comfortable with mistakes at the initial stages in building your business. Decisions can go wrong at any point. Every decision has the potential to grow or sink the business. Most often, the business person does this with limited skills and expertise at the start-up stage. You become better as you continue to grow and mature in your decision-making processes.

Growing up, like many people, we had little resources to start with and a few people to emulate concerning going to school and becoming an entrepreneur.

At an early age in school, I was not sure what I would become but definitely sure of what I did not want to become. I did not want to grow up poor and marginalized. Junior Secondary level was beautiful because I liked school and our teachers encouraged us to study hard so we could have a better future and this depended on how well we passed our examinations. They told us that school had the potential to train us to become Engineers, Doctors, Lawyers, and Teacher etc. I never heard anybody say that school could make me become an employer if I studied well.

At Senior Secondary Level it was all about studying hard in order to become successful in life. Science was what I did because I qualified for it and not because I knew how science was and what I wanted to be, but it turned out to be a good decision studying Mathematics, Physics and Chemistry. Now, most of the theorists in these courses had names that were never familiar in the environment I grew up, and so how would I become an innovator or creator. I could not relate to any of such heroes in science or engineering.

I nurtured hope to be someone prominent in society and to help my family, but I did not know it would take doing business. Who were the heroes in entrepreneurship or the industrialists that I could look up to? Then I passed to the University level to study engineering.

Up until filling in the forms to the University I had not heard of Agricultural Engineering. I had heard of Mechanical Engineering because I knew someone who had done that. I did this course but was not sure of what I was going to do with it after the programme. During my university days, we looked for ways to travel outside the Country to experience most of these places that we had heard about and seen on TV. We were so naive.

If your parents were not in good standing financially, getting the right documents to travel outside the country was tough. Our mates who did not get to the university would find it very difficult to travel to any of these countries that we were fascinated with. Travelling was also part of the reasons people would get to the universities. We did not understand most of these countries that we wanted to travel to and their perception of Africans and the so called opportunities there.

What supersedes this is when you have a vision for your life, because with it you will be willing to go through what it takes to realize the vision. The bigger the vision the better, especially when it is linked to our Country and our Continent and their development. Somebody should have taught us that what life requires is to have a vision to live far beyond livelihood and having a job and that our country needed us to be relevant.

The teaching of African history was not part of our programme and I never saw the need to study history as an engineering student. At the time that we were completing the four year degree programme, most of our year groups irrespective of courses they pursued had the mind to travel outside the Country to look for better jobs or further their education. Those who could not travel had the only option left and that was to look for better jobs which would not come readily, at least not the ones we called decent. The call of duty to help develop our country was not instilled in us. All we knew was to look for jobs and develop a career.

How was modern day education introduced to Africans? Were we introduced to engineering, science, creativity, innovation and entrepreneurship or we were introduced to humanities, arts and social studies?

If we were taught science education without the need for entrepreneurship thinking and development then we would be waiting for another person to employ us. And without teaching us history and its relevance in continuing from where others left, we would not understand what has been sacrificed for us and what we would have to do for the next generation.

It is not that non science education is not important but we are not going to do production through industries if we are not getting the majority coming from our colleges doing sciences balanced with good African history. Taking time to develop the business and leadership skills needed to build a business goes beyond learning science and engineering.

A healthy link among science education, business skills development and African history is what is really needed. My business education started after completing the degree program in engineering. I was inundated with engineering principles and mathematics but no professional training or leadership skills. The University did what they had to do but it was left to me to know what I had and what I did not have to pursue life and develop as an entrepreneur. What helped me was that I was an avid reader of books about business, leadership, entrepreneurship and subjects outside engineering.

After the first degree I had to either look for job or travel. I dabbled with lots of ideas that could be developed into business but stopped and went to do Masters in Engineering. I registered an enterprise after completing national service. Looking for job was not that much on my mind and I was not sure what I was to do with the Engineering.

The practical experience that I had during the short term internship in an engineering firm was not enough for me to start. This lack of industrial professional training makes it difficult for us to start businesses in engineering fields because the exposure is that little. How do you start a business in manufacturing or engineering with no technical expertise? This is the reason most of us start in trading or commerce at the initial stage or you learn to partner with someone with technical skills.

It would take years for me to understand the path I had taken and the kind of person I had to school myself to become to be an entrepreneur from a family and a country background which has little business understanding. All I could hear was go and look for job, and quite frankly where were the jobs and who would even do some introduction for me to get a decent job?

This business journey is lonely and harsh but with the right knowledge and preparation things get better if we don't give up. I have had business ideas that did not work out and business relationships that went bad. I have lost money through bad decisions and bad choices.

It would take time for me to develop the skill-set needed; the leadership skills and character development. I had to learn that companies are able to do well when they start with vision and have the continuous desire to do things rightly.

I had to learn how to lead, develop and inspire a team and be patient with the process till it succeeds. A business should have a vision and solve problems for society and people. The strength to withstand opposition and frustration that comes with building anything significant was part of the things that I had to learn. This generation has the best timing and resources to create business opportunities. We have unlimited access to information. The Internet is a big leverage. There are opportunities in construction, fashion, retail, agriculture, education, entertainment, sports, manufacturing, oil and gas, finance, media, telecommunication, Internet, technology, etc that we can explore.

The need to develop the right mind-set, the business skills and the network is essential and critical, if you want to start your own business. Starting business requires courage and people who cannot stand on their own don't have to be entrepreneurs. We need to have conviction, confidence, and courage to start and build in a growing, but an unpredictable economy. Thus, it takes determination and hard work to build a business.

In some parts of the world, most people start businesses because they see opportunities not because they cannot find jobs. There is the need for us to see opportunities in starting businesses to create jobs, offer better products and services.

The good thing is, finding a market share to grow is not so much difficult. This is because most of our business sectors need improved services, products, systems and organisation. Having to work to gain experience and network before you start any business may come with some advantages in administration, management, and some professional skills. However, they find it difficult to muster the courage, the thickness of skin and the versatility needed at the startup stage.

The level of pessimism that people show towards enterprise and business needs a reorientation. Don't expect family and friends to agree with you when you start; it is even more discouraging for those with so-called degrees. Family and friends will not pride themselves in your endeavour, rather you will be expected to get jobs in multinational companies, get married and start a family. You will be compared with your colleagues who are employed. Entrepreneurship, to them, is not for those who have gone to school and you are in it mainly because you cannot find any job. They will be happy if we succeed.

Majority of people who are doing business are self-employed. They may not have any formal education and the know-how to build companies. They may also lack vision and leadership to attract and develop people to grow their businesses. They even tell their children to look for employment and that they engage in what they do because they did not go to school.

Business has not been part of the educated populace because the educational system has not been structured to produce innovators and creators of industries who embrace the idea of learning to build anything after school. Perhaps, this could be one of the reasons we have many informal business sectors. The closest we get when it comes to entrepreneurship from those who have degrees is about being consultants and self-employed. Building companies require that one develops the mindset to think structurally and learn how to work with a team.

Solving problems is what business is all about and so when we doubt our abilities to solve our problems, we will not have many entrepreneurs or a supporting ecosystem that can develop many business people.

ENTREPRENEURSHIP AND THE
IMPORTANCE OF HISTORY

History well studied and taught has a way of repairing the image of the African. No matter what we teach people, if they believe that they are inferior, cursed or are lost in the culture and image of others, they will live limited lives. We have to believe unequivocally that we are not inferior in our thinking and abilities.

The teaching of African history beyond slavery and colonisation is important in the development of entrepreneurs in Africa. This history should date back to even 5000 years or before. Many people don't even know that such information exists. There is the need for us to research on these epic facts of Africans as entrepreneurs even if we were not taught in our schools. We still think someone is responsible that is why we are looking for help every time or don't see anything wrong with begging all the time. The business person with a vision should not follow this cycle.

We have not been trained to solve the problems of our environment because there is no sense of pride of our heritage when it has to do with building businesses.

The lack of sense of history in our education is partly responsible for this.

Teaching history to engineers, doctors, teachers, etc. gives them a better perspective about the problems, and makes them patriotic enough to look for solutions. This history I am talking about is not about colonisation and slavery, but acquiring the right information on African. It is imperative that we do this because we all have some form of information about who we are, but they are the kinds that make us victims. Education is of little or no use if we can't solve our immediate problems. The current system of education cannot solve this problem.

Teaching, what I call, proper African history, in all programmes will help instill in us a sense of purpose, patriotism and value for people and can hold people to high standards by changing expectations. We will get to know what we have endured and have achieved that was not told us. When people are exposed to their greatness in history, they become proud and bold.

We are hardly taught about our heroes in science, technology and innovation, yet we want Africans to become innovators. The examples we see don't represent us when it comes to achievements.

What we are seeing is the teaching of slavery, colonization, African culture and traditions and calling it African history. They teach our weak moments and leave the great ones. This has made us question our capabilities as a people; this causes us to believe we are incapable of handling our own problems.

Over the years, the image of Africa or the black race has been mutilated. Unfortunately, we have not put any structures in place to amend that. Our misunderstanding of leadership, consumer based thinking, small and selfish thinking, bribery and apathy, all support the fact that we need to build strong mental structures for development. No one can do this for us.

Errors have been promulgated and some think that we use that as an alibi to cover our weaknesses and wickedness. I don't think so. The solution lies in the knowledge of who we are, our talents and passions, our purpose and willingness to stay with our dreams to see them realised. We can repair and amend this image of a needy people at the individual levels since governments or society as a whole may not be able to do this in our lifetime.
We continuously see images of Africans portrayed in every wrong way in most media houses around the world.

Subconsciously, we will need a strong identity to be assertive and not feel limited. We will not be in the position to develop entrepreneurs who are skilled in leadership and character when we have not developed people to be courageous, well informed and confident.

WHERE THE WORLD IS GOING

It will take more effort to train the African entrepreneur in repairing this misconception on self-image and how our continent is viewed by us and the rest of the world. We have different ways of doing things. We operate in a different environment and with different business and governmental structures. We can learn management system from different environments but we need to develop appropriate technologies and techniques which suit our situation in order to succeed.

If we will build a successful and prosperous continent, it is entrepreneurs who will create jobs and build industries. The best that our governments can do is to create the enabling environment necessary for businesses to flourish. This will require a generation that has been prepared to think differently. The business people who are going to help to develop our continent are those who are continuously developing themselves keeping in mind where the whole world is heading in terms of the future, technology and business. Africa will not be the next big thing if our entrepreneurs are not thinking as such.

We still have basic problems that need business solutions in housing, food, clothing, health etc. This calls for business minds that are thinking beyond our immediate needs. We should not just be a consumer market for the rest of the world. We can add value to our products, goods and services.

LONG-TERM THINKING AND PATIENCE

Starting a business does not just happen; our experiences pattern us on the path of entrepreneurship or employment. The path of the entrepreneur can be chaotic. Developing the idea, forming the team, providing the leadership, staying peaceful and strategic when things don't work out as initially planned, and sourcing for funds are all needful.

We started businesses in engineering, construction, fashion retail, etc. with no family business connections, or political network, no capital and no business leadership skills. We started with our belief in God, our belief in ourselves and our belief in Africa. We were not sure of what we were doing but we kept going in the middle of difficulties, oppositions and mistakes. We have resolved not to give up. And we are still moving forward. I dare say that this is the category that most of our graduates find themselves. We need to help people with so little to start to dare to think differently and independently. Business could be their best option.

If we are going to develop the mind-set to start businesses, we have to think differently about problems especially the basic human problems we face in our country and have the vision to solve those that get our attention; the ones we have the skill set to solve. We have to see problems as opportunities and not run from them.

We need to understand that there is a mind-set and skill-set for the entrepreneur. Patiently, we have to learn how to develop the ability to build and lead a team. We also have to understand that building a business is not the quickest way to get money, but the surest way to create longterm wealth.

Constant learning will eventually pay off in our bid to creating jobs and solving problems if we don't give up.

I have attempted to share my thoughts on how we can develop this entrepreneurship mindset.

Your perspective is your reality.
Enjoy the read!

CHAPTER ONE
PERSPECTIVE

* * *

I have a friend who is employed as a barber. On a particular day when I visited him, he was keen in travelling somewhere that he thinks is more developed. I asked him why he is so interested in travelling elsewhere. Just like many people, he believes that he will get a better life when he travels. I would agree with my friend the barber because he has little formal education. I told him if it is about going to visit such places, it is a good idea. But I ached because not many from Africa can

How many of the rich in these countries are Africans?

make any significant change in their lives when they travel abroad. Yes, there are legitimate reasons for people to travel and not every one of them is a bad idea.

> There is nothing like staying with your family in your home country and being involved in the upbringing of your children if you make that your possible option.

My friend, the barber, has confidence in these countries purely because of what he has heard about them which could be true or untrue depending on how one looks at those countries. The richest in these countries are businesspeople who are solving problems. How many of the rich in these countries are African migrants? Africa has produced many successful entrepreneurs.

My friend needs to ask himself these questions; how well he answers them will be his determinant.

1. What is his understanding of his God and the provisions he has made for him? Almost all of us say we believe in God.

2. What is the level of confidence he has in Africa and the opportunities here?

3. What does he know about himself, his passion and abilities?

4. What does he know about business and problem-solving?

The disparity in lifestyle and levels of income has more to do with the mind-set of the individual, their willingness to succeed in life, and their diligence to see through the goals they set for themselves. If my barber friend could tune in to the same thinking in Ghana, nothing can keep him poor. It may take a little longer, but he can still do what he wants to do and possibly get involved in his children's development and have a good family bonding and raise responsible children.

You don't travel to look for a job and think that you will be a millionaire. Almost all the people who travel abroad go there to look for jobs but not to create jobs. Yet,creating jobs is where the opportunities are if we stay commited with the process.

WE NEED MORE THAN DEGREES

In our tertiary schools, people are mesmerised with going abroad while in school or right after school. Some don't even come back when they travel abroad while in school. Majority of us were brought up that way. Some say it is natural for people to go where they can have a better life. I agree to that, but I also believe that a generation can be conditioned, over time, to think in a particular way without questioning it.

> And how are you going to be rich if you are looking for job? You become rich by creating jobs in these countries.

3

START CONTINENTALLY

What you know about the continent is important. If nothing at all, you can read about all the countries in Africa, their population, current economy, the demographics and what business opportunities are there. How are we going to grow businesses in African countries that we know nothing about? Make friends from these countries and continue the conversations. Too many times, we look beyond the continent for partners when we can find many of them here. There are friends from Kenya to Nigeria, Zimbabwe to Togo, etc.

SEE POSSIBILITIES

If you are a student and contemplating entrepreneurship, your education is a plus. We live in the age of information. You can go on the Internet and have a repository of business information. In spite of what you read in school, business talent can work well if you are willing to pursue more.

OPPORTUNITIES

Creating opportunities falls in business more than any other way. It is not about the money, but the good you can do with the money. You can create employment no matter how few the jobs may be.

> It is not about the money per se, but the good you can do with the money.
>
> You can create employment no matter how few the jobs may be.

The leverage an entrepreneur gets is what he becomes if he continues to develop himself at the personal level.

What my friend the barber could have done was to develop his entrepreneurship mind-set and skills. Having the ability to barber is not good enough to build a business. Just as he took time to learn how to cut people's hair, he has to learn how to build his business. If he can register his barbering shop and open bank accounts, he will be on his way to establishing his barbering business. He can start to think of opening more shops and employ others to manage those other shops; he will be providing the leadership needed for the company to succeed. He will not need to travel somewhere to be successful. But it starts with the right thinking. And how will he think it if he does not know it? How will he know if he is not taught?

You will not succeed in a place you don't believe in.

And how will he think it if he does not know it?.

We survive the turbulence and the storm that come with building anything when we build structures; structures are not steel and concrete.

Eventhough these professionals serve society well, many of them spend their lives becoming better barbers, doctors, teachers, lawyers, masons, nurses, engineers, politicians, bankers, etc.; they only upgrade their skills to work to earn more money but they never learn and improve their skills to make money and create

> The one who owns the football team pays the players; he understands how money is created, and the footballer understands how to work for the money. They are different skill sets.

structures to expand. The one who owns the football team pays the players; he understands how money is created, and the footballer understands how to work for the money. They are different skill sets.

The barber works to earn the money every minute and the one who pays him his salary has acquired and developed the skill to create money. Both skills take time to develop and both are technical. Business is technical.

The ability to see opportunities and the strength to take the pain and continue to develop the idea into a business is technical. It takes time to develop it.

> Opportunities are seen when you have developed yourself to see and not by being in any country.

Opportunities are seen when you have developed yourself to see and not by being in any country.

Tough times don't make anybody better, but it is the lessons that tough times bring that make people better; that is if we learn from them. We don't give up on ourselves but we can let go of a business that doesn't work over time or remodel it to work. This is the belief that my friend the barber should have and the patience to develop himself. He should grow from being employed to being self-employed and having the skill to employ other barbers and build a business that manages barbering shops in different locations.

I am not saying that it will be a very smooth journey for my friend establishing himself as an entrepreneur. He will encounter many challenges along the line, but if he keeps going, he will accomplish his dreams as a business owner. The challenges that come with building a business is what most people don't like, but that is the reality of entrepreneurship. We meet many challenges and we become better as we solve them. It is a continuous life of learning to become better.

Business is technical.

There is the need for a business plan, it does not have to be complex. Just make sure you do the major part yourself. The essence is the processes you go through when you are preparing the business plan. Learn accounting terms like cash flow, profit and loss, management account, assets and liabilities. It is important. In the business plan, your management team is key. State the people behind the business idea.

CHAPTER TWO

MINDSET

O ur thinking defines our views of the world we operate in and the size of our vision. Business thrives on the ability to look beyond the present difficulties and launch into the possibilities of tomorrow. What I have seen is that entrepreneurs are occupied with the brighter side of entering into any enterprise.

For a person who has the potential to be employed in a big company, what will make him or her launch a business with no guarantee of monthly pay than to accept the job with guaranteed monthly salary?

The way we think is what separates us from the rest. The family background, education, and the environment that the person grows in contribute to the formation of this mind-set. Being able to transcend ourselves from the unknown to the known requires self-belief.

KNOWLEDGE IS LEVERAGE

Our reading habits shape our world views and our frame of thinking. That is why it is good for us to read about finance, leadership, management, industry and so on if we want to start businesses. If you look at people who have been reading for a while, they exhibit some speed in reasoning and decision-making. We read on:

☐ Finance

☐ Leadership

☐ Team-building

☐ Business

☐ Vision

☐ Strategic thinking.

In essence, we become what we read.

In this age of the Internet, it is now possible for anybody anywhere in the world to access relevant business materials. What are you watching? YouTube is full of videos on business. They may not suit the typical African scenario but there are basic principles that we can glean. The only thing is, much of information on the Internet come from the West with no cultural input from where we operate our businesses. This is where perspective and customisation come to play. If you are prepared, you will know what applies and what does not in our context.

THOUGHTS ARE THINGS

For the business person, unless you are into sports as business, you don't need so much time behind the television watching sports. People become what they consistently watch. So if you are going to be in business, you have to spend some time to watch people who have weathered some challenges in business and now have results. They are the people you should admire. What you listen to shapes your mind-set and your mind-set determines the decisions you make.

The way we think is what separates us from the rest.

If your experiences with money, when you were growing up, were not good, you can carry that into your business life which can have effects on your finances. It did have serious effects on our finances. We had to learn from scratch and it was not good.

Our understanding in building business systems is essential in determining the kind of businesses we can structure.

There is no business without a team and how we are able to replicate our vision and ideas into others is part of building a team. The more we can get the team to see the vision and run as we are running, the better the structures that we can build. The structures are the people, not the physical office building.

MIND-SET SEPARATES VICTORS FROM VICTIMS

We attract what our minds dominantly process. When things don't go as we expect, we should not explain them to our detriment. Always understand that we make many decisions in a day and any can go wrong. We don't beat ourselves to death because of our mistakes. Many times, just one good decision will clear all the mess we may have made in the past years. Don't think as a victim. Develop the habit to see yourself as blessed and equipped to build your business.

If you are prepared, you will know what applies and what does not in our context.

CHAPTER THREE

EDUCATIONAL FOUNDATION

* * *

The essence of school is to equip students with the ability to read and understand, and chart a particular career or professional path. More often than not, students choose courses not based on their natural proclivity to do the things they are passionate about, but based on the job market, good or bad grades, the financial status of their sponsors and

> What you listen to shapes your mind-set and your mind-set determines the decisions you make.

so on. If you are in a situation where you notice that what you are reading to become professionally is not related to the things you do with passion, then you can leverage your ability to read and understand by gathering a lot of information on the area

> **The more we can get the team to see the vision and run as we are running, the better the structures that we can build.**

that you have natural flow for. For instance, if you are reading Agricultural Engineering but you end up showing keen interest in entrepreneurship, gather books in finance, business, management and the products or services you want to enter into and read them. This way, you become equally astute as though you had taken those courses and you will become an authority in the field.

Greatness is in doing what we are gifted to do and doing it well. You need to put in efforts and hours to do what you do and that is where talent is required. When you are in your talent, you don't get tired very quickly. You meet the needed hours by doing what you are passionate about. The long hours that you put in will perfect the talent which will secure continuous performance and delivery.

By this, I am not saying if you are in school, don't study any more in the field you are. Become the best student you could ever be. Preparation for life entails passion and natural abilities in what you will eventually do with your life. Great pianists rehearse. Great footballers train. Similarly, entrepreneurs train and they train by becoming better at what they do.

THE BEST EDUCATION IS IN THE DOING

Entrepreneurship is about doing. *Wisdom begins; understanding establishes and knowledge* moves what has been established to the next level.

Start doing something while you are in school. Do some business while in school. Start practicing where you want to go. I think those who go for degrees start late in life in terms of achieving their dreams if it has to do with business. The best time to start pursuing dreams is in our teens, particularly when it comes to building businesses.

Don't believe so much in the course; believe what you can contribute to society while you are still alive or what you use the course content to do to help society. There are so many who think that going to school will help them find destiny. That is not true. Destiny is found in the heart. Schools and degrees only give us inspirations and a broadened mind which can help to bring out what is in our hearts.

Nonetheless, if you are in school, get the best of grades because that also gives you some confidence in achieving a goal.

In the midst of unemployment and retrenchment, the people with the natural flare for starting businesses must gather the courage to start something. Again, entrepreneurship is about doing.

Often, the people who go to school in our society are more careful in starting businesses, even if they have the interest and the training to be in business. Families and friends want us to go for jobs than starting one, particularly when we have just come out of school. That could be part of the reasons that we have such a large informal business sector. The so-called dropouts easily enter into business because that is the only option available to them.

15

The creativity required for modern business demands trained minds. What people study in school should not restrict them from becoming what is in their heart.

Greatness is in doing what we are gifted to do and doing it well.

Education opens the mind up so that what is in the heart can come out, not the other way round. If this thinking is embraced, the hopelessness among graduates would decimate. People would not go to school for a career but to equip themselves and create their own opportunities. In order to bring what is in their heart out, they will need conscious actions to achieve that.

Education is a major tool for all entrepreneurs as it gives us the leverage to be able to read, write and understand. We should look at educating the people around us either formally or informally. If we are able to reduce illiteracy, we will solve a lot of problems. When educated, every human being becomes better inspired. When people are educated, they get the tools to use information for a better life. This helps us to reduce the level of poverty.

Similarly, entrepreneurs train and they train by becoming better at what they do.

The content of our education has not helped us. The reason is that we are educated without much consideration of the needs of our society. Our education system hardly takes the challenges facing our continent into consideration, but a business minded person looks for problems to solve.

Business needs another form of education which comes by doing.

KINDS OF EDUCATION

There are different kinds of education and each has its relevance.

1. Academic Education

I believe the best time to start pursuing dreams is in our teens, particularly when it comes to building businesses.

This is the kind of education acquired through schooling. It largely does not prepare us to take risk or go the way of business. It is important and imperative, but it has so many limitations, especially the one we are given in Africa. This type of education only creates a pattern for us to follow. That is, complete school, look for job, marry, and live for ourselves

2. Career-Related Education

After academic education, the next kind of education we acquire, by default, is career or professional education. We learn this depending on where we get to work after school. This is essential because that is where we develop our professional work ethics and our technical expertise. Those who did not study technical education at the academic stage can still have the chance to learn anything technical. This is where we get to develop skills that we can leverage on in starting a business; be it finance, manufacturing, agriculture, programming, etc.

> The creativity required for modern business demands trained minds.

3. Family or Relationship Education

This is the type of education where we are cultured into a family and society — where our courage is developed. Our social and emotional skills are developed from this stage. It is so important that we are educated well because it is where we are usually taught values that can help us in our lives. How we take correction and see authority is partly established from this type of education.

4. Faith or Spiritual Education

> Education opens the mind up so that what is in the heart can come out, not the other way round.

Our religious education is more powerful than our academic education because that is where we get our spiritual education and belief systems. It is the determinant of why we do what we do. Humans are spiritual beings. It is where we express our faith and compassion in good and bad times. This is where we develop the strength of our spirit and philosophy. This is why a professor can go to an uneducated religious leader for direction and protection. We express our hope and morals from this kind of education.

5. Health or fitness Education

We can have very good vision but if we are not healthy and energetic, we cannot move around to execute it.

What we eat and why we eat is from the health and fitness education that we have. Knowing how to take care of your body and environment requires education. It has a lot to do with how long we live.

6. Racial or Cultural or Historical Education

This book has attempted to establish the importance of history relating to Africans. If we give Africans all relevant academic education, but fail to do this, we will produce a generation of Africans who will know so much about every thing except themselves. Every well determined race teach their people about their history. Correcting the historic and systemic errors on the African Continent and their descents cannot be overemphasised. It is so pivotal to our development.

7. Personal Education

Every one of us came to this world to solve a problem and God has gifted us accordingly. The onus is on us to find that out and to fulfil it. Our passion and desires are linked to what we have been destined to do on earth. This goes beyond money and status. This is where we get our fulfilment and peace. We do all that we do to live our purpose or destiny. Once it is found, all other things fall in place. Our revelation and growth of knowledge in what we are destined to do grows exponentially. Our wisdom is seen in the area of our purpose and that is where our real expertise is. Our vision is clear when we are in our purpose.

8. Financial or Business Education

The number one instrument in creating wealth is entrepreneurship, which is another form of education. Our level of financial education determines the level of wealth we create and control. No matter the area we operate, if we will be financially sound, our financial knowledge should be solid. We have trained engineers, doctors, accountants, lawyers, politicians, etc. who know little about finance and how it is created except by working for it. This is where nations are controlled and subjugated. If we will create prosperous entrepreneurs, our financial know-how has to be ever-increasing.

There is the need for continuous training on all kinds of topics. This pushes us into serious thinking and conditions us into being great with what we do.

CHAPTER FOUR

THE RELEVANCE OF HISTORY

* * *

It is said that people who don't know where they come from are easily persuaded.

We have to face this: Among all the people on earth, Africans seem to have many struggles. This is partly because Africa experienced what the rest of the world did experience but within a compressed time. Unlike others that systems have been set already for them, both physically and conceptually, Africans have to start from the scratch and this calls for a long memory of greatness in history. The problems appear to be many, both mentally and physically. Some have given up and said that Africa is cursed.

Control is more mental than physical, but freedom comes with self-knowledge.

People work with what they know and so if we don't know much, we cannot do much. The solution is spiritual, some people say. I don't believe it is anything to do with Africa being cursed. We have been taught history that seeks to control us perpetually but if it is not taught rightly by us, we will be subjugated for a long time. Control is more mental than physical, but freedom comes with self-knowledge.

As an entrepreneur, you need to have a good heart and a curious mind. It all starts with the questions we ask within our own environment.

DISCOVERY BRINGS AWARENESS

Reading African history that dates back to six thousand years would help. This may not just be slavery and colonisation. Relevant history on the greatness of the people of the African continent is very much important. This is not to hate others, but you can't go to the global table as a photocopy of other civilisations. We Africans have some good things that have withstood the test of time, like our social life and we have been able to largely live together in spite of all these different tribes.

This is not to hate others, but you can't go to the global table as a photocopy of other civilisations.

> **No body achieves success on a straight path but with a willing heart and a strong mind, we get to do more.**

This is a great achievement. However, where we have not done well is getting enough business people who use science and technology to mass produce our necessities; from health infrastructure to housing, food to clothes, and computers to games. It is not so much that we are poor, it is because we need more innovators who are resolute to do whatever they can and whatever it takes to solve our problems in spite of the oppositions from within and without. Nobody achieves success on a straight path; with a willing heart and a strong mind, we can do more. This is the mind-set that the African entrepreneur needs.

As a businessperson, you must know this history and do diligent study on it. We have not known enough about who we are as a people and what we can do together. I understand we are of the Kingdom of God and we don't belong here when it comes to religion, but we are brought up in a culture and the perception we have grown up with on our environment is very important. Therefore when I say Africans, I am referring to our frame of thinking not the colour of our skin. The enthusiasm we exhibit when it comes to getting visas to some of these countries shows that we are still controlled by mental

> **Therefore when I say Africans, I am referring to our frame of thinking as well, not just our skin colour.**

23

conditioning unleashed on us rather than what we are being taught in our churches. We still have a long way to go.

REPAIR THE CONSCIENCE

People talk of science and technology as the subject for the future. But no tree can grow very tall without deep roots. Relevant history of a group of people is the root they have and that determines how far they can go as a people. They fall on it when there is any opposition. It is important to promote science and technology and the Internet, but without a proper mind-set on history, science and technology will not do much, because most of us still see ourselves in the shadows of others and their misconception on us when it comes to achievement in science, technology, and business.

Entrepreneurs equip themselves with;

The materials they read. They are the determinant. It is good to read academic materials, but the materials from people in business are more beneficial, particularly those from business people who want to see Africa solve her problems and not from the ones who only care about their business and their money.

What they listen to. We live in a country where there is a lot of political discourse on radio. As much as you can, limit the number of times you listen to political talks and listen more to business talks. If you want to be an entrepreneur, pick business topics, buy tapes and listen to them every now and then. That will be a whole school on its own. It is another form of education and it is different.

24

> **You will become knowledgeable because for us to go far, we need to be tough.**

You will become knowledgeable because for us to go far, we need to be tough. The entire social set-up does not normally support you when you start your business.

Not the family, friends nor government can support you, because not many have experienced what it takes to start a business from nothing with no experience or money. It is not that glamorous. The history of ourselves has not made us to believe and patronise what we have produced ourselves. We so quickly embrace what comes from an outsider than what our fellow country people have done. If you don't believe it, just watch the TV. We still have a lot to learn.

OUR GENERATION CAN CONTINUE

I love picking topics and watching them on YouTube. All your favourite authors may have topics that have videos on YouTube. Separate yourself and learn. Continue to learn to build yourself because the contradictory thoughts and self-doubt are many, especially when things are difficult or when you make mistakes, which you will make a lot in life.

> **Civilisation, for me, is the transfer of accumulated information from one generation to the other.**

Civilisation, for me, is the transfer of accumulated information from one generation to another.

> We need entrepreneurs who are patriotic enough to stay here and solve some of our problems.

If we want things changed, then the quality of information we give to the next generation cannot be the same information from the previous generation.

This is especially true when what was handed down to us is not helping us come out with the technologies to solve the daily problems we face as a people. Health problems, unemployment, education, lack of clothes, hunger and so on. Our population is growing every day and so we cannot delay any more. We need entrepreneurs who are patriotic enough to stay here and solve some of our problems. This calls for different thinking.

This is the reason an entrepreneur needs a different kind of education that focuses on problem-solving.

Having talked about the importance of history, we should individually decide what we read to develop our knowledge.

> The continuous improvement of the culture of the people is the drive of growth, and not technology.

Like the majority of our people, I did not get educated thinking that history was wrongly taught, particularly with a university degree. The way history has been taught has made Africans ill-equipped to solve the problems confronting us. We don't know how to build together. We seem to get people who are so much self-focused and this partly explains underdevelopment. History beyond slavery and colonisation can put a lot of things into perspective and that is what happened to me when I got to study the relevance of African history. The continuous improvement of the culture of the people is the drive of growth, and not technology.

The reason an African entrepreneur does not have an appreciation of African history is because he was not taught; he is continually told to malign Africa and our perceived underdevelopment. We are able to use appropriate technology to solve our challenges as Africans when we can see the value of people. We should not be the only person succeeding in our circle.

Government has not provided the infrastructure needed to support start-up businesses. Just look at our tax laws, the interest rates and our procurement procedures.

I have met many of our mates employed with these multinational companies who don't see the need to even engage those of us who are entrepreneurs and believe that we can offer better goods and services. We should know that the onus is on all of us to develop our continent. If we can have some of them to see the need to network with our entrepreneurs to create jobs, it will bring massive improvement. Majority cannot see that big picture of each of us playing our part in building our continent. They are focused on their career without any sense of direction in building the continent. .

We can do better, but we have to be well prepared. It will take self-education and self-development.

Government has not provided the infrastructure needed to support start-up businesses. We have to improve on our laws, the interest rates and our procurement procedures.

Entrepreneurs need to be encouraged to know they can succeed despite the numerous challenges they are bound to face at the initial stage. This can get more people to see entrepreneurship as a tool to developing the continent, creating more opportunities, value, and prosperity.

Our institutions would have to build the capacity of our local companies by giving projects to them instead of prioritising foreign companies.

This will take time to change. It definitely comes with a cost. Each of us must decide what to contribute.

C H A P T E R   F I V E

VISION AND TEAM

* * *

Having a vision has a way of giving us leverage over difficulties. We should expect much from life. Vision requires selflessness and patience.

We can start from our rooms but we should think big and far.

If we want to build businesses, then it will be beneficial to have a vision. Our sense of vision should not be numbed because of difficulties. We can start from our rooms but we should think big and far. Who knows what can happen when we think big?

Making the team own the vision calls for leadership. Until the team owns the vision, it is only your vision. A vision is meant to be shared. Until the team owns the vision, you have not done your job as a leader. We can raise the standards when we train our teams to own the vision. This is so important because outside that, you will have to be present for them to work and when you are not there, not much will be done.

> **Until the team owns the vision, it is only your vision. A vision is meant to be shared.**

A vision starts with the problems that we want to solve. Many people don't have vision for their lives. If you want to run a business, you need to have a vision and be committed to realising it. This is what separates you from those who are only in it for the money. A vision is not meant to make you selfish. Once the vision is about problem-solving, you become relevant. Many people are so self-focused that they care less about the problems facing our country. It is about their livelihood, their career, their family, their children, etc. Unfortunately, this cripples their sense of vision. A vision requires that we add value to lives; all entrepreneurs must be driven by this.

> **A vision requires that we add value to lives; all entrepreneurs must be driven by this**

The process of business development takes time; we should understand the culture and environment that we operate. The resilience that we need to acquire leadership and business skills, patience, networks, and emotional intelligence will need time.

All these are ingredients we will need to be successful. We have to invest in ourselves and have full confidence in people and the dignity they deserve.

When it comes to starting a business, where you come from, your family background, your education and all other social privileges don't matter that much. What matters is your positive outlook of life. Stay positive and be convinced that you have all that it takes to be what you **The reality is in the vision. Don't feel disadvantaged.** envision. The reality is in the vision. Don't feel disadvantaged. Be confident that once you can see it, you can become it and you are ready to develop the skills it will take to achieve it.

You can have a vision but you will need a team to realise the vision. The ability to identify the gifts in people and nurture them is one knack an entrepreneur must have. People will follow you when they see themselves in the vision and it is our job to make this clear to our team. Whenever people are into building anything, it is very dangerous when they don't appreciate the contributions of others. This is a threat to the growth of the relationship. We just have to learn to appreciate one another's contribution and be thankful always. It is the only way we can build together. If you want a good team, you have to be a good team player. If you want great partners,

The ability to identify the gifts in people and nurture them is one knack an entrepreneur must have.

31

you have to be a great partner.

We will not be greater than the team we are able to build. It is said that if you want to go fast, go alone, but if you want to go far, go with a team.

Our inclination to do business alone is so prevalent because it takes a lot of work to be able to work with a team. Some skills are required to lead a team. An entrepreneur should be able to work with a good team; that is where our success lies.

Some skills are required to lead a team.

Many of the successes will depend on the team and when the bad winds blow, we will be saved by the structures of the team that we have been able to build over the long haul.

Being able to work with a team and building networks takes a heart that believes and loves people.

Building a business is about building a team. Being able to work with a team and building networks takes a heart that believes and loves people. This requires patience and self-confidence. Small thinking and negative internal rivalry cannot build a solid team. The best asset of the business is the quality of its people, their exposure and their diversity. The composite creativity of a team is the dexterity in the diversity of its team members.

One of the things you look for in a partner is their confidence, competence, vision and respect for people and ultimately, how they handle defeat and difficult moments. The business will be tested and difficult moments also test us. If the team is committed, no tough moment can stop the vision.

It is key to continuously train your team. For a start-up, it is likely that your first team will not stay with you for long, but you still need the courage to train them. You may not have enough capital to pay them much in terms of salaries but you still have to be open and build a team if you are going to be able to build any company at all. The idea that you have to

The idea that you have to do everything yourself will not build a company.

do everything yourself will not build a company. Your best asset is the quality of the team you have. This will invariably call for consistent training to get the mix that you will need to establish a professional culture that can deliver the results wanted.

You will not be able to lead the team to the level you the leader have not reached mentally.

While training and developing your team, you the leader will also require training and development. You will not be able to lead the team to the level you the leader have not reached mentally.

When it comes to your start-up partners, as long as it depends on you, continue to develop with them and don't let the eventual difficult times or success separate you. You should mature to handle disagreements and look at the big vision that the business can offer.

All these are possible when the partners are fully involved in the business full-time and are committed to its success. You should not have your head in the business while your partners have their legs in it; they should not work part-time while you are working full time. That is always disastrous in my belief.

> **In business, people are the structures. Build the team.**

The potential that entrepreneurship has to change our continent is enormous but it demands deliberate efforts.

In business, people are the structures. When they came for Jesus, they could not identify him because he was not the best dressed or better than his team. There was equity and that is the essence of leadership.

> **When they came for Jesus, they could not identify him because he was not the best dressed or better than his team. There was equity and that is the essence of leadership.**

Some of the issues that you may have to develop the resilience to handle is the reality that people come in and go. Most of them will go in peace without disagreement or fight, but you will have some of them who will never befriend you again after leaving. We have to just get used to the movement of people and be comfortable with ourselves while we use every employee leaving as an opportunity to learn and develop as business leaders. There will be those who will leave and later will want to come back.

My advise is that you will have to think about it well before you take them back. For those who leave because of difficulties, when you take them back and there is trouble, they will leave again.

People who don't respect your leadership don't have to be part of the team, because they undermine the bonding of the team and such people underplay your influence. As much as you can, look for character over degrees. Those who have no history in helping others find it difficult to be good team members; they happen to be very competitive at the personal level.

> Some people will stay with you for a lifetime no matter the difficulties you go through. When things become successful, take good care of such people.

They go for personal glory all the time but a start-up culture does not need that, because your structures have not developed to handle selfish people at the managerial level. Some people will stay with you for a lifetime no matter the difficulties you go through. When things become successful, take good care of such people. People will always come and they will always go, but you should develop a business that will have high retention rate of good people.

CHAPTER SIX

LEADERSHIP AND CHARACTER

＊　　＊　　＊

I n our lifetime, we should have a generation of people who will look at character as the basis of our success. We will not steal and cut corners to get ahead. Not from our country, our employers or families. When we start with good character, we end well. It is the only guarantee for continuous success and this is a timeless principle.

When we start with good character, we end well.

In our entrepreneurial journey, we will be hurt and disappointed by people and we will hurt others too. Some of those who hurt us are people we genuinely help.

Leadership and character have to do with people, their weaknesses and strengths. We should have kind hearts as business people and be wise to build up relationships. Leadership is a skill and it takes time to have it. So is loyalty.

It is imperative that we pursue both intelligence and integrity continually.

Entrepreneurs who are dishonest are building businesses that will not stand when bad times show up. Integrity will keep us. Integrity and intelligence are somehow related. On the road of success and achievement, what separates the men from the boys is how much pressure they can take without losing their focus and peace. Intelligence is also the ability to see the ramifications of our decisions and the power to do it or not. It is more than mental exercise. Intelligence is expressed in skill and delivery. It is important that we pursue both intelligence and integrity continually. Money is not everything.

Business leadership is an art and science. When we develop the required skill set, emotional intelligence, character, and the strength of mind, it shows that we are prepared to do what it takes to be successful.

Let people know and believe that you are trustworthy. There are lots of good things that come your way as an entrepreneur if partners and workers can trust your word.

Let people know and believe that you are trustworthy.

Don't be afraid of losing.

It is expensive to finance a project in our country but once you take people's money to do business, pay back even if you have to start all over again. Don't be afraid of losing.

Leadership is inspirational and it sees the value in people. If we want to be good leaders, we have to be selfless and focus on the reason for the leadership in the first place; which is people.

Leadership is inspirational and it sees the value in people.

Stages and tests that the entrepreneur is likely to go through:

1. The test of the business idea and its viability

This is the stage that proves the viability of our idea. Our ideas are generated based on our exposure and skill set. The business is most likely to fail when the idea is ill-conceived; that is, when the idea is not well thought out.

2. The start-up team, their skill, exposure, emotional intelligence, commitment, professionalism and passion

The strength of the start-up team is so important to the survival of the company. The more diverse the team, the stronger and more committed they will be. Your ability to keep the team together and focused on the vision of the business is a test for you as an entrepreneur. A wrong team will just break the company before it even becomes successful.

3. Cash flow and debt management.

How you handle this is a make or break for the team and the company. This is what I call, finance-debt test. This is a stage which can quickly collapse the business if it is not handled wisely.

Knowing how to borrow and paying it back is important. You need to keenly monitor your finances and how money comes in and out of the business. This I have learned the hardest way and still learning. Looking at our economy and business culture, starting a business in the construction industry where you have to work and accumulate before you are paid is not the best place to start a business if you are not that experienced. The cash flow problems are many for contractors. I have had lots of difficulties in this area; outside construction, our other industries have done better.

But construction is also an area that you can scale quickly if you develop the right business skills and leadership.

4. Government institutions and how to deal with them morally and legally

Learn how to cooperate with public and civil servants lawfully and ethically. Every stage of the business requires certain skills, expertise, and abilities.

Success is linked to your emotional state and internal motivation than your educational or professional experience. The very essence of entrepreneurship is how you handle mistakes and errors; that is everything.

The entrepreneur's job is to deal with uncertainties but how to know, predict and solve uncertainties is so imperative. The satisfaction of building an idea into something that is adding value to lives and creating opportunities is a great feeling.

Business failure is so real and the percentages are so high. In countries that business structures are well developed, the percentage of business failure is still high mainly because of the person starting the business, their leadership and entrepreneurial skills, professional development, their understanding of the industry that they are operating in, the culture of the people, financing, etc.

We have many graduates being churned out of our universities who are without technical skills and professional experiences and yet we want them to start businesses or create jobs for themselves. This normally comes from those who have not really started companies from the ground.

When children are exposed to commerce in the early stages of their lives and devote a lot of time to reading about it, they end up founding their companies. The defining moments come when people spend their time on that which they have been gifted naturally, practicing them and getting proper information on them.

My suggestions will be;

1. Stop the fear of failing in starting any business. Some have tried as many as four businesses before succeeding. You should be looking at doing as many as ten if it has to take you that many times to get the skill of building businesses.

It takes time to build expertise and building a company is not an exception.

2. It is far better starting with partners than to go alone. You may start with a friend or a family member. You may have to do your search well. Look for their stress tolerance level, their expertise, their outlook of life and the inclination to the vision of the business. However, it is better to go alone than to go with a wrong team. If the team is wrong, the business will fail before you even start

3. Register the business, and open a bank account. You will need good relationship with your bankers. Most people might think you are in business because you are not able to find a job. Their perceptions will change when you start to succeed.

4. Don't over think and over analyse; it is a sign you are not ready yet. It may show that you are so afraid of starting. Entrepreneurship is about doing.

5. Get a website, create a social media presence, and your room can serve as an office. Don't worry so much with getting an office to start. The money to rent an office can be used for the first order.

6. Be straightforward and honest in your dealings. This is your biggest competitive edge. If people can trust you, you will go places. Don't change what makes people trust you when you see success.

7. Don't be afraid of the mistakes and controversies that come with building a company. They will come but they don't have to kill your dream and passion.

8. Talk to the tax office, the social security, and all other relevant governmental agencies. This is because you will deal with them along the way.

9. Create partnership and be resolute not to get in shady dealings. You exchange the wisdom and the muscle that you need as an entrepreneur when you are making shortcuts.

10. When you borrow money, make it a point to pay back no matter the difficulties. Debt management is part of the lessons that you will have to learn. We have to learn to pay back our loans and how to use credit to build the business. Some people don't agree with this and it is okay. But it is an acceptable practice to learn how to use good debt to build businesses.

11. You will need lawyers, accountants, IT, human resource professionals along the line. But remember it is still your call and your business.

12. Read articles on business, leadership, finance, the industry you are in, etc. It is a life-long commitment.

13. Go for excellence in all your dealings. We can go with our culture and our identity but we cannot sacrifice the quality and the excellence that is required around the world.

14. Learn how to raise capital from your customers, partners, investors, etc. It is a crucial skill and it does not come that swiftly.

15. Find people who are doing it and learn from them. Not those who are writing articles about entrepreneurship, but those who are doing it with character. Their wisdom is always invaluable.

Leadership is required to build structures and teams to handle growth. There is a vision, the leader, and the team. Leadership is influential and inspirational or it is not leadership.

Leadership is influential and inspirational or it is not leadership.

The population is ever increasing; we need more entrepreneurs to produce food, shelter, clothing, water, energy, etc. No other group can do it for us but ourselves. The love for the people, sense of purpose, sense of vision, and the sense of history can produce that generation who can solve our problems.

CHAPTER SEVEN

BELIEVE IT

* * *

The convictions of people determine what they become in life. Our beliefs, what we say about what we believe, what we see about our beliefs, and ultimately what we do about what we believe changes every situation.

A person can have great talent but if the talent is not exposed to an environment where discovery of the talent can happen, the person's greatness may not be discovered. Entrepreneurship is discovered through appropriate training and and nurturing.

> **Entrepreneurship is discovered through appropriate training and nurturing.**

Discipline and courage from the entrepreneur is needed for the business to survive. The passion for business, as any other talent, is like a magnet which attracts any magnetic material in its field. Whatever is in you attracts the very future you are to become.

We don't make permanent decisions based on the temporary difficulties. Life is more than what we will eat, wear, or where to sleep. We need to have purpose. We have to make our own world and that decides how we carry our vision around. What is important is preparing for the future we want. We don't wait for the future. We prepare for it. Our preparation today is the future we have.

Whatever is in you attracts the very future you are to become. Your future is in you.

DEVELOP YOUR TALENTS

It is important that you find what you are good at and cultivate it in knowledge by reading and practice by doing. Some of us may have more than one talent but there will be one dominant talent; develop that one first. What is it that you do with ease and cannot stop reading or talking about? That may be your talent and that is where your greatness is.

What is it that you do with ease and cannot stop reading or talking about it?

Upgrade your knowledge in the field of your interest. You cannot change what

46

you don't know. Therefore, be voracious when it comes to knowledge, particularly knowledge in what you do. Leaders are readers and those who read will end up leading.

Therefore, be voracious when it comes to knowledge, particularly knowledge in what you do.

If you don't see your future in what you are discussing, you will need another set of friends and relationships. Most of your friends should be people who are interested in building businesses and who are ethical and credible. You need friends who have good self-esteem. They will be happy for you when you succeed

You need friends who have good self-esteem.

YOUR RELATIONSHIPS DEFINE YOU

You cannot be an entrepreneur when all your friends are looking for jobs. You will be discouraged because your mistakes will be overblown. You need people who are going where you are going so that you can discuss the journey. If they are not building businesses, it will be far from them.

DON'T WORRY ABOUT THE MISTAKES

Enjoy your way up. You may not have deviated but there are stages and processes in building anything. Similarly, building a company from the ground has stages and processes.

Be determined not to give up and decide to enjoy the ride. You are going to make lots of decisions but not all of them will work out as expected. Don't beat yourself too hard because of the mistakes you make; they will bring out the immaturity in you quickly. What matures us is the frequent corrections of the mistakes that we make. If you are determined, you will become better in your decision-making and build a profitable company that will be an expression of what you stand for.

Your ability to handle what I call debt-pressure is so key. The mistakes you make and the ones by your employees or partners will become debt or loss to the company. The way you handle the people you owe, be it employees, bankers, individual creditors and partners is very much important. Always be respectful and communicate frequently. Respect and communicate with creditors openly. It is important when there is non-payment on your part and don't crumble because it is a stage that you will come through.

> Don't beat yourself too hard because of the mistakes you make; they will bring the immaturity in you quickly. What matures the entrepreneur is the frequent corrections of the mistakes that we make.

The pressure is not so much the problem. It is your stamina and your strength to handle the pressure. That will qualify you to the next stage of your development.

Always be respectful and communicate frequently.

Not knowing how to handle loans is not a good thing but most of us will go through it because of the limited knowledge we have when we start. If you are going to handle major businesses or projects, you will need financing along the line and so it is imperative that you learn to work with it. If you have made mistakes in this area of financing as an entrepreneur, don't be beaten, fight back and you will win. Don't run away from your creditors, even those who threaten your life, take you to court or insult you. Come out as someone who has been prepared for all stages of business life. You need to think beyond houses and cars; you are creating opportunities that we so need.

Don't run away from your creditors, even those who threaten your life or insult you.

CHAPTER EIGHT
START

* * *

U nemployment is a major issue, but it is not among those who engage themselves beyond the academic works while in school. It is a bit easier to figure out what to do with your life when you are engaged with your vision. If you are ever going to work after school, why put it on hold till you are through with tertiary education?

WORK TO LEARN

We become skillful in whatever we start to do early and entrepreneurship is no different. If you experienced commerce in your up-bringing, you would show interest in business.

If you ever helped someone in their business while growing up, you will develop interest in business. One of the reasons why we don't have many people with good work ethics is because we don't start to work early. Most people's first employment is national service but that is very late.

In helping people who are entrepreneurs, it has to do with training. Everybody has a talent which can be developed into business with the right training. This is where mentorship is required; learning from those who have done it.

Entrepreneurship is a talent that when discovered early in life, must be developed with the right information. It is like a footballer exhibiting talent in football and being exposed to somebody who recognises the talent and channels it rightly. The fellow can then end up in professional football with proper training and exposure.

> Entrepreneurship is a talent that when discovered early in life, must be developed with the right information.

Additionally, the training must not just centre on the products or services that the businessperson is interested in, but being equipped with leadership and team-building skills, and setting out the vision for the business. These may be translated in knowledge on a particular business, finance and cash flow management on how the business is carried out.

Spending time in nurturing your skills on business development is as imperative as the talented footballer training to become a professional.

> With no business education, no professional education and little technical skill but insanely ambitious, I have kept trying to build companies in a business environment that is not so structured.

I have done many things that I never considered business, growing up. Not many of them I ever thought was building a company, from agriculture to retail to construction and transport. There was never a clear way to start and not many mentors to learn from. This increased the number of mistakes I would eventually make trying to understand what I would have to become to be an entrepreneur. It is a life-long learning. Knowing what business to do, learning how to source for money to get a contract done, learning how to borrow and pay back even if I did not make any profit, and who to partner with without being cheated or screwed were among the lessons I had to learn.

There are so many con men and women who you will meet as you grow your business. With no business education, no professional education and little technical skill but insanely ambitious, I have kept trying to build companies in a business environment that is not so structured. Huge interest rates, non-payment of works done and delays in payment with start-up employees who put in just a little to get by, I have learned that to build a business, the mission has to be more than just trying to get money.

My love for God, people and country has kept me going in the middle of so many difficulties and this is the reality of trying to build businesses. The difficulties should bring the best in us but not to stop us from building what we believe we have been called to do. There is inner peace and tranquility that will come from upholding the principles of love, honesty, patience and respect.

Ambition separates people. Ambition decides what people are passionate about and how they spend their time. Ambition separates the strong from the weak.

No matter how small it is, start something. Continue to renew your strength and update yourself. You don't need money to start your business. You need money to build it, but not to start it. Businesses are started with ideas, and so you should not let lack of money stop you from starting. We have started businesses without money, but it requires stamina to continue to grow. You don't need to listen to the people who say it cannot be done. Start from where you are.

CHAPTER NINE
DIFFERENT TIME

*   *   *

M any do not know what to do after completing college and one of the most obvious choices available is to travel abroad to seek greener pasture. We therefore pursue post graduate courses in countries we go and hope to develop professions. Very few Africans move from Africa to anywhere in the world to become entrepreneurs. We go there to look for jobs. There is nothing wrong to look for jobs in these countries but if you want to be an entrepreneur, then go there and start businesses.

> Very few Africans move from Africa to anywhere in the world to become entrepreneurs.

Your choices or the ones made for you might have ended you abroad. But the thinking that those who are abroad have more opportunities is not true. The world has really changed and probably the only thing that has not changed may be your thinking about the possibilities and opportunities in Ghana, and for that matter, Africa.

It has little to do with "I have come with money, what business can I do?"

People who have been employed all their lives abroad come home to Africa and they want to start businesses. Then the reality of entrepreneurship hits them. Most move back that quickly. Entrepreneurship is not just about making money, it is more of a course and wanting to build a vision. If you come and start business and you were never into business, you will go through the processes of entrepreneurship development; what should keep you going should be your belief in the idea that you are building. It has little to do with "I have come with money, what business can I do?" Even if you were doing business somewhere, you will still need to learn how to do business in the African environment, the behaviour and work ethics of the people, government laws, etc. It takes patience, skill development and high sense of purpose to develop.

In life, the desire to fulfill your destiny must propel you more than the search for greener pastures. Your destiny is tied to helping and lifting people; where else needs human capital development than Africa?

56

Nothing determines the course of a nation than the mind-set of its citizenry.

Now, it is about the tools you use and how technologically inclined you are. Television stations are beaming from Africa to the rest of the world, websites have been built in Africa which are accessible all over the world. The only limiting factor is our mind-set. How far you can see depends on how much investment you have made in yourself. It is no more where you live.

It is no more where you live.

When it comes to business, financial success and increase, what religious institutions have been teaching people cannot produce success at the individual level.

Religion can largely help in the development of character and morals, but not the technical know-how that is needed in entrepreneurship.

Teaching people religious issues cannot replace the technical skills development that building business requires. Just as going for religious programmes cannot turn anybody into an engineer or a doctor, so going to such programmes cannot produce successful entrepreneurs. Religion can largely help in the development of character and morals, but not the technical know-how that is needed in entrepreneurship.

Many have not seen business as a field which requires order and organisation and so we term the things we don't understand as spiritual. Growth occurs with proper orderliness and that is where many small-scale business people fail.

Having another source of revenue is not entrepreneurship. It is more than the money. It is a call.

There are principles of growth. If you are going to be hugely successful in anything, particularly as a business person, you will be required to do some of these things;

1. Come in early and be the last to leave.

2. Develop your talent with knowledge.

3. Be loyal and honest.

4. Be committed and persistent.

5. Think big.

6. Treat people well.

7. Don't be occupied with the criticisms from those who don't know how to start business and grow it.

8. Have fun.

9. Don't fear mistakes and failure, they are part of the process.

10. The invisible that causes the increase is God and His principles.

C H A P T E R T E N
ESSENTIAL

* * *

The size of our spirit determines our future. How well we have prepared, and how far we can see are very essential. We should have a can-do spirit all the time. Feeling sorry for ourselves when things go bad is not the attitude to have as businesspeople. If you are spiritual and an entrepreneur, that is also a legitimate course which is relevant. Entrepreneurship is an art and science which requires development. We go into all the world, including the world of

If you are spiritual and an entrepreneur, that is also a legitimate course which is relevant.

entrepreneurship. Many understand being employed or working to get extra revenue but not building business with a vision. Few know this.

Our faith makes us strong. That same faith builds us courage and strength in times of trouble. Our spirituality builds us and we become better. It gives us advantage and clear direction to keep going when others give up.

> Our faith makes us strong. That same faith builds us courage and strength in times of trouble

It is from our spirit that we exhibit love, humility, trust, hope, honesty, loyalty, perseverance, patience, intelligence, wisdom, understanding, knowledge and all the virtues that are sought after in the business realm. This is how you win.

Every gift God has given us is in our spirit and our business talents are in our spirit as well. From our spirit, we get the wisdom to make the right business decisions. The more mature our spirit becomes, the more quality business decisions we make and the more profit and increase we see. Fear causes businesspeople to make wrong decisions.

> Every gift God has given us is in our spirit and our business talents are in our spirit as well.

What we are taught as spiritual people affect our decisions and choices. The life of the entrepreneur is not superstition. Running around all the time to prophets to get the interpretation

The life of the entrepreneur is not superstition.

of why your business is not doing well is not the way to go. People do this while they have not even taken time to understand the structures and processes required to have a successful business.

For many, business is another way of getting revenue and so if the revenue is not coming, then there is a demon that must be cast out. There is the God-factor and that factor demands organisation and structure. There is the Wisdom of God and there is the Power of God. There is diligence as well. Therefore if you can improve your understanding of what it takes to build a business, then you may not go around to seek spiritual meaning of some of the basic stages that businesses have to go through. We should focus on becoming better entrepreneurs.

Entrepreneurship is such that until we have been one, it is very difficult for us to put things into perspective, because what people call business is really another avenue of getting revenue. But business is mainly a vision with a leader and a team with all kinds of systems and structures to

Entrepreneurship is such that until we have been one, it is very difficult for us to put things into perspective, because what people call business is really another avenue of getting revenue.

make that vision bring value to people. If that is done rightly, revenue will start coming in if you don't give up.

If you are a spiritual person, the background of the one who is teaching you is so important.

What a leader who was unemployed will teach you about the difficulties you meet in your business is different from a leader who was employed in the government sector, or the one who was a politician or an academician or a corporate person. You have to know where to seek teachings when it comes to business or you will be miserable and frustrated and blame yourself all the time; it is an area rarely understood.

Spiritual books are great business leadership tools and you can build emotional stability by devoting more time studying them. Your business or your entrepreneurship journey becomes better when you become a better person. Man is a spirit, he lives in a body and he has a soul. All the three must be working perfectly. Business process development is that daunting and you can become a crook if you don't have your spiritual foundation rightly set. This happens when we are eager to impress people that we have succeeded; *but you don't need to impress others. Just stay with the process.*

> Spiritual books are great business leadership tools and you can build emotional stability by devoting more time studying them.

The businessperson takes advantage of bringing in time and resources from other people to create opportunities and money. Even though the businessperson brings in lots of wealth than the average employed person possibly, the business person must still be able to invest their resources well.

It is normally said that God is our source, which I absolutely agree with, but God needs to have a channel to bring the money to you. Every source has a medium. For me, the medium is likely to be how strategically you can get prepared and position yourself for the blessing that the source (God) brings to you.

It is normally said that God is our source, which I absolutely agree with, but God needs to have a channel to bring the money to you.

AFTER WORD

We need to get many of the people looking for jobs to start thinking about entrepreneurship as a profession. This is not only with those in the IT industry, but agriculture, construction, real estate, retail, transport, logistics, finance, etc.

The idea of college dropouts starting businesses and that you don't need to go to school to start a business may be true somewhere but not necessarily in Ghana or Africa. You can start but without education growth is limited. Things have been structured such that to be able to write or read for commerce or technology, you need to have been to school. However, by the time we complete school, we lose the urge to be ambitious and courageous to follow our dreams outside looking for jobs, which don't exist.

The times require it now, that we prepare people to see starting businesses as the way that we are going to solve the problems we have such as unemployment and poor infrastructure. The process of entrepreneurship development takes time and our entrepreneurs must understand the culture and environment that we operate and the resilience that we need to acquire the leadership skills, business skills, patience, networks, emotional intelligence and all the things that we will need to be successful. Self-esteem and courage are needed. We have to invest in ourselves and have full confidence in people and the dignity that we deserve. Pride in the continent and its history.

It does not have to be slavery and colonisation and looking for help all the time.

Decide to continuously develop your team and treat them with respect. Be honest and don't focus on only the money. We are the ones to build the country. Around the world, people are creating opportunities with entrepreneurship; we can do same. We have access to the Internet, let's create good products and services and not wait for the government to help us all the time. We need to see opportunities outside the government. We can do more for government when we have proven what we can do for the country. We don't have to wait for handouts from government. Be responsible for your life. The government may never come through for you.

We can take advantage of the Internet. It is a great learning and business tool. Start your business and don't worry about the mistakes because you are going to make many of them. Don't worry about the kind of business you start, especially if it is your first business, your best may not even come from your first business, but the subsequent ones will not come if you don't start.

Stay positive and be convinced that you have all it takes to be what you have to be. The reality is in the vision. Don't feel disadvantaged. Be confident that once you can see it, you can become it and you are ready to develop the skills it will take to become it.

Thank for reading this book.

NOTES

....

....

....

....

....

....

....

....

....

....

....

....

....

....

....

....

Made in the USA
Las Vegas, NV
21 June 2025

23900483R00056